by Sunita Apte
illustrated by Mick Reid

SCHOOL PUBLISHERS

Copyright © by Harcourt, Inc.

All rights reserved. No part of this publication may be reproduced or transmitted in any form or by any means, electronic or mechanical, including photocopy, recording, or any information storage and retrieval system, without permission in writing from the publisher.

Requests for permission to make copies of any part of the work should be addressed to School Permissions and Copyrights, Harcourt, Inc., 6277 Sea Harbor Drive, Orlando, Florida 32887-6777. Fax: 407-345-2418.

HARCOURT and the Harcourt Logo are trademarks of Harcourt, Inc., registered in the United States of America and/or other jurisdictions.

Printed in the United States of America

ISBN 10: 0-15-351085-4
ISBN 13: 978-0-15-351085-4

Ordering Options
ISBN 10: 0-15-350603-2 (Grade 6 On-Level Collection)
ISBN 13: 978-0-15-350603-1 (Grade 6 On-Level Collection)
ISBN 10: 0-15-357981-1 (package of 5)
ISBN 13: 978-0-15-357981-3 (package of 5)

If you have received these materials as examination copies free of charge, Harcourt School Publishers retains title to the materials and they may not be resold. Resale of examination copies is strictly prohibited and is illegal.

Possession of this publication in print format does not entitle users to convert this publication, or any portion of it, into electronic format.

2 3 4 5 6 7 8 9 10   179   12 11 10 09 08 07

"Winning is everything!" That's my sister's favorite saying. Of course, it's easy for her to say that. She always wins at everything. Games, sports, spelling bees—you name it, and she wins it. Everything she touches turns into a victory. At least, that's the way it seems to me.

Allow me to introduce myself. I'm Sonia, sister of Susan, winner of everything. Me, I'm just ordinary. I almost never win. Sure, sometimes there's a fluke, and I squeak by with some glory. Still, in general, I try hard and don't get very far, just like most of the other kids I know.

Okay, I admit I'm good at something. I'm a good writer. However, there's no contest involved in putting words down on paper. Our school doesn't have a writing team, not that I wish it did. When someone else tries to write a good story and it doesn't turn out well, I just feel bad for them. I think that might be part of the problem. I don't really enjoy winning. It makes me uncomfortable.

Susan claims that's a defeatist attitude. "How can you ever win if you think you don't like it?" she always asks me. "You've got to get over that. There are winners and losers in life. Which would you rather be?"

A loser, I guess? Okay, I know that's the wrong answer, but it's how I feel. Maybe it's not that I want to be a loser. I just don't want to play the game.

That is why our school's field day is always such a problem for me. Field Day at Ridley Middle School is one giant competitive drama. Each grade goes out on the field to run races and play games. It's a dog-eat-dog day of joy and agony.

I dread it! I dread the three-legged race and the ring toss. I dislike the potato sack relay and the wheelbarrow sprint. Most of all, I can't stand that I have to have a partner—a partner for every race. This partner depends upon me to do well since we get scored together. This partner, I don't get to choose.

It would be fine if I could pick my own partner. That's because my best friend, Rachel, feels just like I do. She couldn't care less about winning. Rachel and I would make great partners.

However, friends aren't allowed to be partners on Field Day. The teachers want to "broaden our horizons" and "take us out of our comfort zones." They get together and choose our partners for us. Usually, my partner is the person I've talked to the least during the school year.

Last year, it was Travis Evans, star of the Ridley basketball team. I think I can safely say he didn't enjoy being my partner.

"Hey, Sonia," he would say after every race or game. "Don't you want to win? You don't even look like you're trying. What's wrong with you?"

"Nothing," I would mutter, as Travis glared at me. It was as if I was committing treason or something.

"I'm trying," I would say half-heartedly, as he shook his head in disgust.

By the end of the day, Travis had stopped speaking to me. That didn't make life much different than it usually was except that before he didn't speak to me because he didn't know I existed. Now he didn't speak to me because I had let our team down. Out of disappointment, he had basically decided to disown me as a teammate.

We stood together at the Field Day awards ceremony. As his buddies clapped and cheered about how well they had done, Travis looked like he was about to cry. I felt bad that he was so upset, but I wouldn't have cared otherwise. I mean, no one gets ahead in the real world by winning three-legged races. What does it matter if someone is good or bad at them?

Susan, however, felt differently. "How could you do that to poor Travis Evans?" she asked when she heard. "You know winning is very important to him."

"Susan, I *did* try," I pointed out.

She shook her head. "Obviously not hard enough. You're not bad at sports. You just don't care."

With that, she tossed her head and walked off, making me feel small the way only big sisters can. I knew my attitude embarrassed her. She just couldn't understand why I didn't want to win.

I thought it over. Maybe she was right. I owed it to my Field Day partner to care more and vowed that this year's Field Day would be different.

I would care. I would be a winner!

However, the world works in mysterious ways. This year on Field Day morning, when the partners were announced, I got a big surprise.

"The next pair will be Sonia Rogers and Alex Cabrera," a teacher called out.

Alex Cabrera? He was the new kid in our grade. He kept to himself and was extremely shy. In fact, no other sixth grader had ever heard him speak. If there was ever a sixth grader who appeared to be less of a winner than me, it was Alex. We were going to make quite a pair.

Out on the Ridley field, everyone chatted loudly. Partners had to wear the same colored T-shirts, which the teachers handed out. Alex and I got yellow ones, not a good sign, since people sometimes think yellow is for cowards, not winners.

First up was the potato sack relay. Each set of partners was a team. Alex went first, moving so slowly in the potato sack, he looked as if he was sleepwalking.

"Come on," I yelled, cheering him on. "Go faster. You're almost there. Just a little more, Alex. Okay, now rush back."

As I grabbed the baton and put on the potato sack, Alex looked decidedly unhappy. I didn't pay too much attention. I was rushing out to finish the race. I hopped as fast as I could in my sack. Alex and I were going to win, we were going to be winners, we were going to be…

Losers! We came in last in our group. By the time I hopped back to the starting line, all the other teams were sitting down.

"I'm sorry," I said to Alex. "I tried as hard as I could." I was depressed. I had finally cared enough to try, and I was still a loser.

Alex gave me a funny look. "Why are you sorry?" he said. "I don't care."

That was the most I had ever heard Alex speak. I was so surprised that for a moment, I didn't really register what he had actually said.

Then it dawned on me.

"You mean you don't care if we win?" I asked.

Alex smiled. "Not at all," he said. "Winning a race isn't important to me. I have other things I enjoy that I'm good at."

That intrigued me. "Like what?'

"Like creating murals. I'm doing a big one on the back wall of the art room. If it wasn't for Field Day, I'd be finishing it today."

Suddenly, I realized Alex and I suited each other as Field Day partners. It was strange because this year, of all years, I had convinced myself to care about winning. I didn't have to do that anymore.

I began to laugh. Alex looked confused.

"What's so funny?" he asked.

"I don't care whether or not we win either." I was still smiling. "I thought you cared, so I was trying really hard to care, too."

Now Alex began to laugh. "Wow, we're the perfect partners," he said.

I linked my arm through his. "Yes," I agreed. "We are."

I realized that I had finally rejected Susan's idea of the world. She thought there were only two groups—winners and losers. Now I knew that there were three groups—winners, losers, and those who don't care about winning.

For the rest of Field Day, Alex and I had a great time. We tried very hard to come in last at everything. We almost made it, but the terrible team of Krista Wolcott and Derek Jones beat us to last place in the three-legged race. I guess you can't win them all.

Think Critically

1. Why does Sonia dislike Field Day?

2. How are Sonia and Susan different?

3. What is Alex's attitude about winning? Why is it important to the plot?

4. How can you tell that Alex is a good artist?

5. Are you more like Sonia or Susan in your attitude toward winning? Explain.

 Health

Field Day Chart Plan a field day for your school. What events would you include? Make a chart of the events. Then write under each event how it could help participants improve their physical fitness.

 **School-Home Connection** Discuss the book's plot with an adult at home. Talk about attitudes toward winning and losing in sports you know.

Word Count: 1,372